Artists in Profile
HARLEM RENAISSANCE ARTISTS

Denise Jordan

Heinemann Library
Chicago, Illinois

Designed by Tinstar Design
Printed in China

07
10 9 8 7 6 5 4 3

Library of Congress Cataloging-in-Publication Data
Jordan, Denise.
    Harlem Renaissance artists / Denise Jordan.
      p. cm. -- (Artists in profile)
    Includes bibliographical references and index.
    Summary: Discusses the characteristics of the Harlem Renaissance art
      movement which flourished in Harlem, New York, in the 1920s and presents
      biographies of eleven artists.
ISBN 1-58810-649-7 ISBN 978-1-58810-649-0
1. African American artists--New York (State)--New York--Biography--Juvenile literature. 2. African American art--New York (State)--New York--20th century--Juvenile literature. 3. Harlem Renaissance--Juvenile literature. [1. Artists. 2. African Americans--Biography. 3. Harlem Renaissance. 4. African American art. 5.
Art, Modern--20th century.]   I. Title. II. Series.
N6538.N5 J67 2002
700'.89'9607307471--dc21
2001005437

Acknowledgements
The author and publishers are grateful to the following for permission to reproduce copyright material: Cover photograph by permission of New York State Office of General Services, Harlem State Office Building, NY, NY; pp. 4, 6, 47, 48 Photographer James VanDerZee, copyright Donna Mussenden VanDerZee; p. 5 by permission of New York State Office of General Services, Harlem State Office Building, NY, NY; pp. 7, 11, 16, 17, 22 Schomburg Center for Research in Black Culture, Art & Artifacts Division, The New York Public Library; p. 8 Schomburg Center for Research in Black Culture, The New York Public Library/Art Resource, NY; pp. 9, 43, 51 Schomburg Center for Research in Black Culture, Prints & Photographs, The New York Public Library; p. 12 Whitney Museum of American Art; p. 14 Gibbes Museum of Art/Carolina Art Association; p. 18 Beinecke Rare Book and Manuscript Library/Yale University; pp. 21, 25, 32 Smithsonian American Art Museum; pp. 27, 31 Harmon Foundation/Still Pictures Branch, the National Archives at College Park; p. 28 San Francisco Museum of Modern Art; p. 35 Courtesy Scurlock Studio Records, Archives Center, National Museum of American History, and Schomburg Center for Research in Black Culture, Prints & Photographs, The New York Public Library; p. 36 Milwaukee Art Museum; p. 39 Chicago Historical Society; p 40 Ackland Art Museum, the University of North Carolina at Chapel Hill; p. 44 Howard University Gallery of Art, Washington, D.C.; p. 52 Hampton University Museum, Hampton, Virginia; p. 54 The Phillips Collection, Washington, D.C./The Jacob and Gwendolyn Lawrence Foundation; p. 55 Schomburg Center for Research in Black Culture, Art & Artifacts Division, The New York Public Library/copyright Romare Bearden Foundation/Licensed by VAGA, New York, NY
Photo research by Dawn Friedman

Some words are shown in bold, **like this.** You can find out what they mean by looking in the glossary.

Contents

What Was the Harlem Renaissance?

The Harlem Renaissance was an artistic movement that took place in Harlem, a neighbohood in New York City. The time period is debatable. Some scholars say the Harlem Renaissance was a single decade, beginning in 1920, and ending in 1929. Other scholars disagree; they believe the Harlem Renaissance continued into the late 1930s. This book focuses on the years from 1920 to 1929. A unique group of artists, thinkers, and **patrons** was active in New York City during these years. These artists, thinkers, and writers fought hard to make African-American art visible to a large audience. They changed the way the world viewed African-American art and artists.

The New Negro Movement

The Harlem Renaissance developed from the New Negro Movement, a deliberate, national effort to redefine the African-American community, called the Negro community at that time. In the early years of the 1900s, African Americans were trying to overcome inaccurate stereotypes that described black people as ignorant, lazy, untrustworthy, and unlovely.

The New Negro Movement was formed to use art, philosophy, and literature as tools to destroy the wrongful **stereotypes.** The authors, thinkers, and artists of the New Negro Movement had four main themes: using Africa as a source of pride, honoring African-American heroes, encouraging racial and political change, and recognizing African-American traditions.

The UNIA Parade, by James Van Der Zee (1924)
James Van Der Zee, a Harlem Renaissance photographer, took this photograph of a parade organized by the Universal Negro Improvement Association (UNIA). The UNIA was interested in many of the same ideas as the New Negro Movement.

W. E. B. Du Bois (1868–1963)

W.E.B. Du Bois was born in Barrington, Massachusetts. His mother died soon after he graduated from high school. Du Bois got a scholarship to Fisk University. Du Bois graduated from Fisk and enrolled at Harvard University. He earned another bachelor's degree at Harvard, then a master's degree, and a Ph.D. in sociology.

Du Bois is best known for his work with the National Association for the Advancement of Colored People (NAACP). He helped establish this civil rights organization in 1909. He served as public relations officer for the NAACP and editor of *Crisis* magazine. Du Bois was known as the voice of the NAACP.

Du Bois believed the best way to change people's minds was through art and literature. His book, *The Souls of Black Folks*, was instrumental in drawing attention to the problems that faced African-Americans.

The New Negro Movement gained strength after World War I. Before World War I, most African Americans lived in the rural South. Many of them worked on farms. When the war began, manufacturing industries grew to support the war effort. Many African Americans went north. They found work in factories in cities such as Detroit, Pittsburgh, and New York. They spread the word that jobs were plentiful and that working conditions were better in the North. Soon many people were moving to the northern cities.

The mass movement of people from the outh to the North is called the great migration. The great migration was an important theme for Harlem Renaissance artists. Langston Hughes wrote poems about it, and Jacob Lawrence created paintings about it.

▌▌ *The Subway*, by Palmer Hayden (c. 1930)
Hayden painted the new way of life for African Americans who moved to the northern cities.

Harlem: the center of African-American culture

The great migration route led to New York City and Harlem. People moving from the South stayed with family members in Harlem until they could afford a home. They settled in Harlem close to family and friends.

Black businesses grew. Actors, singers, and other entertainers arrived. Political and social organizations like the National Association for the Advancement of Colored People (NAACP) and the Urban League also moved into Harlem. The NAACP was founded in 1909 by a group of activists. They wanted to improve education, housing, and transportation. The Urban League formed in 1910 to help African Americans adjust to living and working in an urban environment. The NAACP's *Crisis* magazine and the Urban League's *Opportunity* magazine provided work for black writers and illustrators. Artists, writers, and intellectuals moved to Harlem. Harlem became the cultural center for black America, and the place where white America discovered black culture.

As Harlem became a center for black culture, people began to associate the ideas of the New Negro Movement with Harlem. More people were aware of the artists, writers, and thinkers in Harlem who were creating work based on the New Negro philosophy. People began to call this period of new African-American ideas, art, and literature "The Harlem Renaissance."

Portrait of Couple with Raccoon Coats and Stylish Car, by James Van Der Zee (1932)
Harlem was the home for a new, middle-class group of African Americans. The couple in this photograph were proud of their success, visible here in their fashionable coats and car.

■■■ *Jockey Club*, by Archibald J. Motley (1929)
Both African Americans and whites were drawn to the nightclubs in Harlem. These clubs supported musicians such as Duke Ellington and made jazz music popular. Soon, this new music form was common all over the country.

The beginning of the Harlem Renaissance

The NAACP helped create the Harlem Renaissance in 1914, by offering an award. The award, called the Spingarn Medal, honored an African American who achieved success in religion, science, philosophy, or business. In 1924, the NAACP awarded the first Spingarn medals for fine art. The medals encouraged African Americans to use their own cultural background to create art.

In 1922, William E. Harmon, a wealthy white businessman, established the Harmon Foundation. In 1928, the Harmon Foundation gave awards for "distinguished achievement among Negroes." The awards rewarded achievements in literature, music, fine arts, business and industry, science and invention, education, religious service, and race relations. After the contest, the foundation exhibited the art submitted for the fine arts award.

Because of prejudice, the mainstream art world did not take African-American artists seriously. African-American artists were not accepted in many art schools. Because of this, it was hard for them to get their work displayed in galleries and art museums. It was difficult to sell their work. The Harmon Foundation exhibits generated interest in creating, displaying, and buying African-American art.

The Great Depression, the WPA, and Harlem Renaissance artists

The Great **Depression** began after the crash of the New York stock market in 1929. People lost large sums of money, businesses closed, and millions of people lost their jobs. There was no extra money for people to spend on art.

Government programs were created to provide work for the unemployed. The Public Works of Art Project (PWA) started in 1933. The PWA **commissioned** artists across the country to create art for public buildings such as libraries, courthouses, and schools. This program ended in 1934, but the Work Projects Administration (WPA) replaced it from 1935 until 1943. The WPA Federal Art Project paid artists about $50 a month. Harlem Renaissance artists fought hard to be included in the Federal Art Project. They created art for public buildings and taught in community art centers.

Art of the Harlem Renaissance

The art of the Harlem Renaissance is not abstract. It reinforces the tradition of storytelling in African-American culture. The art tells a story about the lives and the history of African Americans. Family life and urban scenes are common themes.

OPPORTUNITY
A JOURNAL OF NEGRO LIFE

JUNE
1926

The Harlem Renaissance helped African Americans achieve visibility and respect as artists. The Harlem Renaissance artists fought hard so other black artists could attend art schools and exhibit their art in museums and galleries. Many of these artists became teachers who passed the ideas of the New Negro Movement down to the next generation.

▮▮ *Opportunity* magazine cover by Aaron Douglas, 1926
Artists such as Douglas came to Harlem to work with the other African-American artists, writers, and thinkers.

Alain LeRoy Locke (1886–1954)

Alain LeRoy Locke was born into a wealthy Philadelphia family. He graduated with highest honors from Harvard University. He was the first African-American Rhodes Scholar.

Locke taught at Howard University in Washington, D.C. He served as a mentor for young artists, introducing them to people who could support them as they struggled to produce their art. He also worked with the Harmon Foundation, developing prizes in literary and artistic achievement.

In 1925, Locke wrote an essay titled "The New Negro." He described the new negro as an educated, cultured, and patriotic American. Later, he produced an expanded version of "The New Negro." The new version included poetry, fiction, and art developed by Harlem Renaissance writers and artists.

■■ *Opening Night, Lafayette Theater,* by James Van Der Zee, 1929
This photograph was taken just before the stock market crashed in 1929. At the time it was taken, Harlem was a successful neighborhood, supporting lots of different businesses, nightclubs, and restaurants. After the stock market crash, people could no longer afford to support the businesses and the arts.

9

Richmond Barthe (1901–1989)

- Born January 28, 1901, in Bay St. Louis, Mississippi
- Died March 5, 1989, in Pasadena, California

Key works
African Dancer, 1932
Blackberry Woman, 1932
Stevedore, 1937

Richmond Barthe learned to draw when he was a little boy. "When I was crawling on the floor, my mother gave me paper and a pencil to play with," said Barthe. "It kept me busy while she did her errands."

Barthe was born on January 28, 1901, in Bay St. Louis, Mississippi. His parents were Richmond Barthe, Sr. and Marie Clementine Robateau. A few months after Barthe was born, his father died. His mother took in sewing to support her family.

When Barthe was six years old, his mother married William Franklin. His mother and stepfather encouraged Barthe to make art. Other people also noticed Barthe's interest and ability in drawing. Barthe remembered that he was about six years old when "a lady my mother sewed for gave me a set of watercolors." He said, "By that time, I could draw pretty well."

In the summer, William Franklin delivered ice. When Barthe was old enough, he helped his stepfather with the deliveries. Mrs. Lorenzen, one of the ladies on the ice route, did not like to see Barthe working on the ice truck. She helped him get a job with a wealthy friend, Mrs. Harry Pond, so that he would have time for his art. When the Pond family moved to New Orleans, Louisiana, they took Barthe with them.

Barthe continued to draw and paint while he worked for the Ponds. Around 1923, he painted a picture for a church festival. The minister at the church, Father Jack Kane, admired Barthe's painting. Father Kane was angry to learn that local art schools would not admit Barthe because he was black.

Father Kane arranged for Barthe to attend the School of the Art Institute of Chicago, one of the few art schools in the United States that accepted black students. He paid the tuition for the first year, but Barthe was responsible for his own living expenses. Barthe got a job as a waiter to earn the extra money.

Barthe made two important contacts at the School of the Art Institute of Chicago: Archibald Motley, Jr. and Charles Schroeder. Motley was another black student. Schroeder was a teacher. He taught Barthe how to draw the human figure. Schroeder also encouraged Barthe to try sculpture.

"One day ... he asked me to do a couple of heads in clay, saying that they would give me a feeling for a third dimension in my painting ... I did heads of two classmates, one male and one female. They turned out so well, I **cast** ... them and they were shown during 'The Negro in Art Week,'" explained Barthe.

Barthe got good reviews on the sculptures. He also got a few **commissions.** Barthe was asked to do a **bust** of Henry O. Tanner and a bust of Toussaint L'Ouverture. Tanner was an African-American artist. L'Ouverture was a Haitian military hero. Barthe stopped painting and focused on sculpture.

Richmond Barthé, by Robert Savon Pious (1938)
This portrait of Barthe was painted by Robert Savon Pious. Like Barthe, Pious studied art at the School of the Art Institute of Chicago.

11

Henry Ossawa Tanner (1859–1937)

Henry Ossawa Tanner was creating art long before the Harlem Renaissance, but he influenced many Harlem Renaissance artists. They were inspired when they saw his work in magazines or museums. African-American artists studying in Paris visited Tanner's studio for advice.

Tanner was born in Pittsburgh, Pennsylvania, on June 21, 1859. He attended the Pennsylvania Academy of Art and the Academie Julien in Paris, France. Disillusioned with the racism and discrimination he faced in the United States, Tanner decided to stay in France. He died in Paris, France, on May 25, 1937.

Later, Barthe attended an exhibition in Gary, Indiana, that featured four Jubilee Singers, members of an African-American musical group. When Barthe returned home, he cast the head of one of the singers. It was called *The Jubilee Singer.* This sculpture appeared on the cover of *Crisis* magazine.

Barthe was asked to do a one-man show in New York but he said no. He needed more practice and time to develop more pieces. Barthe went to the Art Students League in New York, another school that accepted black students. He submitted a sculpture to the Harmon Exhibition in 1929 and received an honorable mention.

In 1930, Barthe exhibited 40 pieces at the Women's City Club art show in Chicago. Based on this work, Barthe received a **fellowship.** The money from the fellowship allowed Barthe to continue to study sculpture.

Barthe had his first one-man show at the Caz-Delbo Gallery in New York in 1931. It generated a lot of excitement among art critics. They called Barthe's work "sensitive" and said his sculptures communicated the feelings of his subjects.

In 1933, Barthe displayed some of his pieces at the Chicago World's Fair. Later, an exhibition was arranged at the Whitney Museum of American Art in New York City. The Whitney Museum purchased three of the Barthe's pieces: *Blackberry Woman, African Dancer,* and *The Comedian.*

In 1939, the Baltimore Museum of Art hosted a showing of African-American art. This was the first time a museum in the South had held such an event, and Barthe was one of the artists chosen to participate. He showed a new piece called *The Stevedore.*

When the United States entered World War II, Barthe was asked to help with recruiting efforts. The government wanted to encourage African Americans to fight in the war. Barthe agreed to help and completed several military sculptures. Barthe's recruiting efforts kept him busy, and he could not work on his other art. He was not selling many pieces, and he was losing money.

Sculpture became more **abstract** during the war. When the war ended, Barthe was no longer popular. The reviews for his next show said his art was old-fashioned. The show and the poor reviews made Barthe depressed. Most of his friends had left New York, and he felt isolated. When a friend invited Barthe to Jamaica, he went.

Barthe started painting again in Jamaica. During the 1960s, American colleges and organizations rediscovered Barthe's work and held receptions in his honor. When people found out where he was living, they went to Jamaica to see his work. Soon, so many people were visiting Barthe's home in Jamaica that he could no longer work there. In 1969, Barthe moved to Switzerland and then to Italy. Barthe stayed in Italy for several years. He began to feel lonely. He decided to go to California, where his sister lived.

In 1977, Barthe moved to Pasadena, California, and did not have much money. A journalist interviewed Barthe and told his story to actor James Garner. Garner met Barthe and secretly arranged to pay his rent. Pasadena named a street after Barthe, and friends established a scholarship in his name. In 1981, Garner held an 80th birthday party for Barthe.

In 1986, Barthe sculpted his last piece, a **bust** of Garner. A few months later, Barthe became sick. He died on March 5, 1989, at age 88.

Blackberry Woman, by Richmond Barthé (1932)
   Barthe was one of the first black artists to sell his sculptures to museums. This piece belongs to the Whitney Museum.

13

Aaron Douglas (1899–1979)

- Born May 26, 1899, in Topeka, Kansas
- Died February 2, 1979, in Nashville, Tennessee

Key works

Emperor Jones Series, 1926
Study for God's Trombones, 1926
Aspects of Negro Life, 1934

Aaron Douglas learned to draw as a child. Douglas's mother was an artist. He spent hours watching her draw and paint. Then, he began to imitate her.

Aaron Douglas was born on May 26, 1899, in Topeka, Kansas, to Elizabeth and Aaron Douglas Sr. His parents encouraged education. Douglas spent a lot of time reading and dreaming about visiting towns far away from Topeka.

Douglas was not sure what he wanted to be when he grew up. He wanted to be a lawyer, but he also wanted to be an artist. Douglas prepared for both careers by taking the hardest classes offered by his high school. In his senior year of high school, he decided he would study fine arts in college.

He had to earn the money to get to college, so he found a job at the Union Pacific Materials Yard while he was still in high school. Douglas graduated from Topeka High School in 1917. A short time later, he and a friend named Edward Foster caught the train to Detroit, Michigan, to find jobs in the automobile factories.

Douglas and Foster had to sit in the baggage car on the train ride. Other seats were available, but they were not allowed to use them. There were other African-American passengers riding with them. Like Douglas and Foster, they had been recruited to work in the factories. These people could not change their minds and leave the train early. If they tried, armed guards stopped them. The companies that had hired them had paid for their train tickets, and they wanted to make sure these people would show up to work.

Douglas worked at the Fisher Body Company building. His job involved mixing and carrying mortar. Douglas had to quit this job because he was not strong enough for the heavy lifting it required. He went to work at the Cadillac factory for two months.

While Douglas was living in Detroit, he visited the Detroit Institute of Art. He found out the museum's staff offered evening art classes free of charge. Douglas went to the art classes three or four times a week while he lived and worked in Detroit.

Douglas and Foster left Detroit and went to New York City. They worked in a glass factory sweeping up broken glass. Douglas managed to save $300 and buy new clothes for school.

Douglas arrived in Lincoln at the University of Nebraska late. School had started ten days earlier. He did not have any of the documents that he needed to start school. The chairman of the fine arts department accepted Douglas into the program on the condition that his documents would arrive shortly. Douglas found a job as a bus boy to help with expenses.

▌▌ *Aaron Douglas, by Edwin Augustus Harleston (1930)*
Harleston was an artist and activist who worked with Douglas on a series of murals at Fisk University in Nashville, Tennessee.

World War I interrupted Douglas's studies. He expected to be drafted, so he joined a unit called the Student Army Training Corp (SATC). He was one of very few African-American students in the corp. A few weeks later, he was told his services were not needed.

Douglas believed he was excused from the Corp because he was black. He left Nebraska after only one semester and went to Minnesota. He attended the University of Minnesota in Minneapolis until the war ended. In his free time, he visited the Walker Art Center to study the art. When the war was over, he returned to the University of Nebraska. He graduated from the University of Nebraska in 1922.

Finding a job was harder than Douglas had imagined. He waited tables until he got a teaching job at Lincoln High School in Kansas City, Missouri. Teaching did not allow much time for creating his own art. He had a few friends in the area, but there were no other artists. Douglas was lonely.

He spent lots of time reading about art. He studied the works of Pablo Picasso and his use of **Cubism.** He studied the German **Expressionist** painters, and he studied the works of Henry O. Tanner. These influences began to show up in his art.

In 1925, Douglas quit teaching. He wanted more time to spend on his own work. Following the advice of friends, Douglas went to Harlem. He found work immediately. Charles S. Johnson, the editor of *Opportunity* magazine, asked Douglas to design some covers for *Opportunity*. W.E.B. Du Bois hired Douglas to design and sketch for *Crisis* magazine.

Aspects of Negro Life: An Idyll of the Deep South, by Aaron Douglas (1934)
*The Work Projects Administration **commissioned** Douglas to create this mural. You can still see it at the Countee Cullen branch of the New York Public Library. Douglas pressured the WPA to give work to African-American artists.*

Langston Hughes (1902–1967)

Langston Hughes was an important poet and writer of the Harlem Renaissance. Some of his most important works are: *The Weary Blues* (1926), *The Ways of White Folks* (1934), *Shakespeare in Harlem* (1942), and *Fields of Wonder* (1947).

Hughes was born in Joplin, Mississippi, but he grew up in Cleveland, Ohio. He was elected class poet in grade school and was senior editor for his high school yearbook. He briefly attended Columbia University in New York City.

Shortly after Hughes arrived in New York, he visited Harlem. In Harlem, Hughes met W.E.B. Du Bois and Alain Locke. Both men were influential to Hughes's career. Hughes also formed friendships with Aaron Douglas and writers such as Countee Cullen and Zora Neale Hurston.

Douglas became well known for his magazine and book illustrations. He designed some book jackets for popular authors. Some of his work at this time included *The Crucifixion*, 1927, for a book called *God's Trombones*, and a cover for *Crisis* magazine.

The 1925 Harlem issue of *Survey Graphics* magazine had a big impact on Douglas. It featured the art of Winold Reiss. Douglas liked Reiss's art. He was impressed with the way Reiss drew on his German background. The men met through Charles Johnson, and Douglas studied with Reiss for two years.

In 1926, Douglas married Alta Sawyer, his high school girlfriend. Many artists, writers, and scholars of the Harlem Renaissance met in Douglas's home. They talked about the issues affecting African-American writers and artists. The idea for *Fire!!*, a Harlem literary magazine, may have originated from one of these discussions.

Wallace Thurman edited *Fire!!* Aaron Douglas did the drawings, and authors including Langston Hughes wrote essays and poetry. There was only one issue of *Fire!!* The magazine failed, but Douglas's illustrations impressed Thurman. Douglas was hired to illustrate Thurman's 1929 book, *The Blacker the Berry*.

In the late 1920s, Douglas began to work on murals. He did his first mural for Club Ebony in New York City. Next, he painted murals at Fisk University in Nashville, Tennessee, and at the Sherman Hotel, in Chicago.

In 1931, Douglas decided it was time to study in Paris. He started classes at the Academie de Grande Chaumiere. Douglas did not like it there. The working space was too small. He left and enrolled in the Academie Scandinave.

Douglas made arrangements to meet with Henry O. Tanner. Other African-American artists were in Paris, also, but Douglas did not see them very much. He wanted to make the most of his time in Europe and studied and worked extremely hard.

The United States was involved in the Great **Depression** when Douglas returned home. He had used up most of his money in France and needed to find work quickly. He signed on with the Public Works Administration and began a set of murals for the Countee Cullen branch of the New York Public Library. These murals were the *Aspects of Negro Life* series.

Sometime during this period, Douglas began to study Marxism. Marxism is a form of **communism,** based on the writing of Karl Marx, a German philosopher who lived from 1818 to 1883. Douglas believed an unequal balance of power existed between blacks and whites. He thought Marxism, which demanded social equality, might make things fair.

Douglas's career changed in 1937, when he agreed to teach art at Fisk University. He started teaching part-time while he worked on getting his master's degree at Teachers College of Columbia University in New York. He received his masters degree in 1940, and by 1947, he was a full-time professor. He retired from Fisk in 1967.

Douglas was a well-respected speaker on African-American art. His work appeared regularly in exhibitions. Aaron Douglas, sometimes called the "father of black American art," died on February 2, 1979, in Nashville.

▌▌▌ *The Prodigal Son,* by Aaron Douglas (1926)
This illustration is included in God's Trombones. The images that Douglas created for that book show stories from the Bible placed in modern settings. This scene is in a Harlem nightclub.

Palmer Hayden (1890–1973)

- Born January 15, 1890, in Widewater, Virginia
- Died February 18, 1973, in New York, New York

Key works

The Schooners, c. 1926
The Subway, c. 1930
The Janitor Who Paints a Picture, 1939
The John Henry Series, 1944–1947

Palmer Hayden left his hometown of Widewater, Virginia, and moved to Washington, D.C. He wanted to be a commercial artist. He placed this ad in a paper: "Young artist would like job as assistant to commercial artist."

Hayden got a response, and the artist wanted to see examples of Hayden's work. Hayden put his best drawings in his portfolio and went to the interview. When he arrived, the artist took one look at Hayden then shut the door in his face. Hayden refused to let this experience stop him. He would find a way to be an artist.

Palmer Hayden was born Peyton Cole Hedgeman in Widewater, Virginia, on January 15, 1890. He was one of ten children. His father, James Hedgeman, farmed, fished, and did odd jobs. His mother, Nancy Bell Cole, cared for the children. Hayden started drawing in school. He drew what he saw around him; cows on the hillside, ships on the bay, and activity in the dockyards. As he got older, Hayden began to think about art as a career.

At the age of seventeen, Hayden moved to Washington, D.C. He tried for a job as an artist's assistant, but he did not get the job because he was black. Hayden did not stop trying. He worked at various jobs to make money to pursue his art. He even joined the circus.

Hayden worked with a group of men to put up the circus tents. He helped with other things as needed. When his work was done, he got out his drawing pad and sketched. He drew pictures of clowns, riders, elephants, and the crowds of people visiting the circus. He made extra money drawing publicity pictures for the performers. He left the circus in 1910. Hayden worked in a brickyard, deckhand on an oyster boat, and then did odd jobs until he joined the army in 1911.

Hayden's name changed to Palmer C. Hayden when he joined the army. Hayden had to ask the timekeeper from his last job to write him a reference. The busy timekeeper was irritated by the interruption. He quickly wrote the reference, handed it to Hayden, and went back to work.

Hayden was dismayed when he was named "Palmer C. Hayden, U.S. Army Private." He realized that the timekeeper had put the wrong name on the reference. "I was afraid to tell them, and afraid to go back," said Hayden. He was assigned to the black unit, Company A 24th Infantry Regiment.

His first tour of duty took him to the Philippines. While there, he made drawings of his friends and the people and places of the Philippine Islands. He was discharged in 1914 but reenlisted almost immediately because World War I had started in Europe. He joined a black **cavalry** troop stationed at West Point in New York. He remained there until the war ended. He made numerous sketches of the soldiers and people in and around the area.

Hayden left the military in 1920. He worked night shift at the post office so he could take art classes at Columbia University. Five years later, Hayden was moved from the night shift to the day shift, forcing him to paint in the evening. The lighting was bad at night, so Hayden skipped work to paint during daylight hours. He was fired for missing so much work.

The Janitor Who Paints, by Palmer Hayden (1937)
Hayden painted this self-portrait while he worked for the Work Projects Administration.

Hayden moved into Greenwich Village, a small artist colony in New York. He met another artist from Virginia, Cloyd Boykin. The men talked about the difficulties that went along with being a black artist. Hayden learned that he was not the only one struggling. Both men did odd jobs, cleaned houses, and did janitorial work to make a living.

One of Hayden's employers was Victor Perard, an instructor at Cooper Union, a famous art school in New York. Sometimes Perard gave Hayden free art lessons. He took Hayden to his home in New Jersey for weekend painting trips.

One summer, Hayden attended the summer art colony run by Asa E. Randall in Boothbay Harbor, Maine. Hayden worked for Randall in exchange for tuition. "That was the real turning point for me," said Hayden. "I began to realize things, to make better connections about everything."

■ *Harbor Traffic*, by Palmer Hayden (1926)
Hayden was interested in painting everyday life. In this painting, he shows men at work in the harbor. Hayden was familiar with work on the water, since he had worked on an oyster boat.

Another turning point for Hayden was a small moving job. He helped a friend move furniture for a wealthy homeowner. The friend had to leave early, but Hayden stayed to finish the job. The homeowner, pleased with Hayden's work, hired him to clean and dust her home. Hayden discussed his desire to be a painter with her. In 1926, the woman told Hayden about the Harmon Awards. Hayden submitted a painting and won first prize. He used the prize money to travel to Paris in March 1927 and enrolled in the Ecole des Beaux-Arts.

Hayden stayed in France for five years. He made several visits to Henry O. Tanner and studied art at the Louvre. He paid close attention to the various techniques in composition and color. Hayden exhibited paintings in a group show at the Salon des Tuileries in 1930 and the American Legion Exhibition in 1931.

Hayden was in Paris while the Harlem Renaissance was going on in New York. He sent paintings back to the United States to Mary Brady of the Harmon Foundation. Brady exhibited and sold some of the paintings. The Great **Depression** had begun when Hayden returned to the United States in 1932. The 42-year-old Hayden got a job at the Harmon Foundation packing art and setting up exhibits. He was also featured in a movie produced by Brady, called *How to Paint a Picture.*

In the late 1930s, Hayden signed on with the Works Project Administration. The officials did not want to hire Hayden, because they wanted to give the jobs to friends or to white artists. However, Hayden had won a Harmon medal, and he was an army veteran, so the officials had to hire him. He was assigned to the easel project, which allowed him to paint at home. He produced *The Janitor Who Paints* and a series of New York waterfront scenes.

In 1940, Hayden married Miriam Hoffman. He was still working for the WPA. He spent time talking with young artists. They talked about their search for black heroes, and Hayden became interested in painting heroes.

Hayden visited Talcott, West Virginia, where the John Henry legend originated. He took notes and made sketches around the Big Bend Tunnel that John Henry helped to construct. He also made a series of paintings about John Henry between 1944 and 1947. By 1950, many artists were exploring **abstract** art. Hayden refused to go abstract. He liked to tell a story in his work. He said, "I paint what us Negroes... or us Americans know. We're a brand-new race, raised and manufactured in the United States."

Palmer Hayden died in the Manhattan Veteran's Hospital in New York City on February 18, 1973. He was 83 years old.

Malvin Gray Johnson (1896–1934)

- Born January 28, 1896, in Greensboro, North Carolina
- Died October 4, 1934, in New York, New York

Key works

Swing Low, Sweet Chariot, 1928
Negro Masks, 1932
Self-Portrait, 1934
Roll Jordan, Roll, c. 1930

Malvin Gray Johnson's career as a painter did not last long. When the 38-year-old Johnson died, the art world lost one of the most influential and promising artists of the Harlem Renaissance.

Malvin Gray Johnson was born January 28, 1896, in Greensboro, North Carolina. Like many other African-American families with roots in the South, Johnson's family migrated north. Johnson grew up in New York City. Johnson wanted to be an artist. His parents could not afford to send him to art school, so Johnson worked to earn the money himself.

By the time Johnson was 25 years old, he had saved enough money to pay for a year of school. He started classes at the National Academy of Design (NAD) in New York City. After he completed the first year, Johnson had to drop out, find work, and save more money for the next year's tuition. It took him six years to complete the program. Johnson graduated in 1927.

After graduation, Johnson found work as a commercial artist. In his spare time, he painted pictures of the people around him and scenes he remembered from his childhood. He also painted several pieces that were based on African-American religious songs, called spirituals.

In 1929, Johnson entered the painting *Swing Low, Sweet Chariot* in the Harmon Foundation's competition. *Swing Low, Sweet Chariot* was Johnson's interpretation of the African-American spiritual of the same name. Johnson was awarded the Otto H. Kahn prize for best painting and $250 in cash.

As Johnson studied the works of other African-American artists and other art forms, he began to try new techniques. He experimented with color and light. He studied African artists and noted the influence African sculpture had on European artists. He studied the work of Paul Cézanne, enjoying the way

Cézanne reduced objects to basic shapes like cubes, cylinders, and squares. Johnson's work became more **abstract.**

In the summer of 1933, Johnson took a painting trip to Brightwood, Virginia, to document the lives of southern black people. He sketched and painted rural African Americans working in fields, in churches, and on prison chain gangs. He painted the Virginia countryside. Sometime during this period, he got sick. He was weak when he returned to New York, but he could not take a rest. He had to prepare to open his first one-man show at Delphic Studios.

The Harmon Foundation sponsored a project documenting the struggles of African-American artists on film. Malvin Gray Johnson was one of the featured artists. A few months after the documentary, *A Study of Negro Artists,* was completed, Johnson was dead.

Malvin Gray Johnson died on October 4, 1934. His death shocked his friends. They made sure the Delphic Studios exhibition went on as planned.

In 1939, the Baltimore Museum of Art hosted an exhibit of African-American art. Johnson's *Self-Portrait,* was included in the collection. His work was highly praised.

Examples of Malvin Gray Johnson's work are valuable today and can be seen in museums across the country. However, much of his work was lost after his death, because museums at the time did not think it was important to keep the work of a black artist.

■■■ *Self-Portrait,* by Malvin Gray Johnson (1934)
Johnson was interested in Cubism and African sculpture. This self-portrait shows the influence of both of those styles.

Sargent Claude Johnson (1887–1967)

- Born October 7, 1887, in Boston, Massachusetts
- Died October 10, 1967, in San Francisco, California

Key works
Sammy, 1927
Elizabeth Gee, 1927
Mother and Child, 1932–1933

"I had a tough time in the early days. They didn't give me much of a chance. They didn't know who I was, but I had made up my mind that I was going to be an artist."

Life was hard for Sargent Claude Johnson. Johnson struggled with discrimination, and he struggled with his desire to become an artist. Few people believed art was a realistic occupation for a black man, but Johnson was determined to achieve his goal.

Sargent Claude Johnson was born on October 7, 1887, in Boston, Massachusetts. His mother, Lizzie Jackson Johnson, was African American. His father, Anderson Johnson, was Swedish. The family experienced racism and discrimination because of the Johnson's **interracial** marriage.

Johnson's father died when Johnson was ten years old. His mother, who was sick and weak, had difficulty managing six children. She sent them to live with her brother in Washington, D.C.

Johnson's uncle was a high school principal. His wife, May Howard Jackson, was a sculptor. Johnson watched his aunt as she sculpted. Soon, he was trying to **model** pieces of his own.

After a while, Johnson and his siblings were sent to live with their grandparents. He did not forget the lessons he learned from his aunt. He continued to practice modeling at his grandparents' house.

When Johnson was fifteen years old, his mother died. His grandparents were old. The care of six active children was too much for them. Other relatives were not willing to adopt the Johnson children. The children were separated— the boys were sent to a Catholic orphanage in Massachusetts; the girls were sent to a school in Pennsylvania. Johnson was able to maintain contact with his brothers for a while, but he never saw his sisters again.

Johnson could sing and play the guitar. He drew well and he continued to model with clay. He took up painting while he was recovering from a long illness. Johnson had to rest for long periods and painting helped to occupy the time.

When Johnson left the orphanage, his teachers suggested he should study music. He went to Boston planning to study music, but he realized he preferred art. He found a school where they taught drawing and painting in the evening. Soon, he quit music school to go to art school.

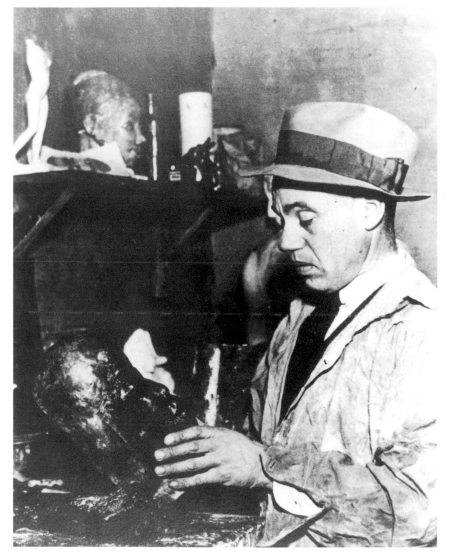

▪▎▎ *This photograph of Johnson shows him sculpting in his studio.*

In 1915, when he was 28 years old, Johnson moved to San Francisco and enrolled in the A.W. Best School of Art. He met and married Pearl Lawson this same year. Johnson worked at several different jobs to earn money while he developed his art. He worked tinting photographs in a photography studio, and he worked as a framer in a frame shop. When he was not working or spending time with his wife, he worked on his art.

In 1919, when Johnson was 32 years old, he entered the California School of Fine Arts. He spent two years working with Ralph Stackpole and one year working with Beniamino Bufano. Stackpole and Bufano were two of the most famous sculptors living on the West Coast.

Living in California allowed him to observe and study art from different cultures—Aztec, Mayan, Asian, and Native American. Each culture influenced him. He tried new techniques, and he experimented with adding color to his sculptures. Johnson also became more aware of his African-American heritage. He read Alain Locke's essay, *The New Negro*. Johnson wondered how to best represent that part of himself in art.

In 1923, Johnson's daughter, Pearl Adele, was born. He started drawing and sculpting children. He produced a study of Pearl Adele in **terra-cotta**. Johnson entered this piece in the San Francisco Art Exhibition and won a medal. He also sculpted a portrait of Elizabeth Gee, a Chinese girl who lived next door.

Elizabeth Gee, by Sargent Claude Johnson (1927) *This piece is typical of Johnson's art during the 1920s.*

In 1928, Johnson entered a ceramic portrait titled *Sammy* in the Harmon Exhibition. *Sammy* won the Otto Kahn prize for Best of Show. The prize included a $250 cash award. Two years later, Johnson won a bronze medal for another piece entered in the Harmon exhibition. In the 1933 Harmon Exhibition, he entered another piece. Again, he was declared a prizewinner.

Johnson received national recognition in 1935 for his piece, *Forever Free*. *Forever Free*, a wood sculpture of a black mother with her arms around two children, earned Johnson the San Francisco Art Association medal for sculpture. This piece was donated to the San Francisco Museum of Modern Art.

While Johnson was receiving recognition for his art, things were deteriorating at home. His wife was in the early stages of a mental illness, and they were not getting along well. In 1936 she left, taking Pearl Adele with her. As time passed, her mental condition worsened. She was hospitalized in the Stockton State Hospital until her death in 1964.

By 1936, the country was in the midst of The Great **Depression.** The Work Projects Administration (WPA) developed a program for artists called the Federal Art Project. When the new program started, Johnson was one of the first artists hired. He was given the position of senior sculptor but was quickly promoted to assistant state supervisor.

The nice thing about working for the WPA was that Johnson had all the materials he needed. An added advantage was that he had a large space to work. For the first time, he could sculpt some large pieces.

Johnson's first large piece was a carved organ screen for the California School for the Blind in Berkeley. Blind children running their hands over the redwood carving can feel the shapes and textures of the animals and people carved in it.

Johnson wanted to go to Mexico and Asia and study art forms there. When he was awarded the Abraham Rosenberg Scholarship in 1944 and 1949, he was able to go to Mexico. In 1958, a **patron** financed a trip to Japan. In each country, Johnson studied art and considered how the artists' religion influenced their art. He continued to experiment with different techniques.

Sargent Claude Johnson died of a heart attack on October 10, 1967, in San Francisco. He was 80 years old. In 1971, a major **retrospective** of his work was held at the Oakland Museum.

William H. Johnson (1901–1970)

- Born March 18, 1901, in Florence, South Carolina
- Died April 13, 1970, in New York, New York

Key works
Self-Portrait, 1929
Jacobia Hotel, 1930
Jim, 1930

"I am no ordinary American Negro painter or no ordinary American Painter, I am recognized by known Americans and Europeans as a painter of value so I must demand respect," William Henry Johnson wrote to Mary Brady in 1937. Johnson spent most of his life in an attempt to earn the respect he demanded.

William Henry Johnson was born in Florence, South Carolina, on March 18, 1901, to Alice and Henry Johnson. Henry Johnson worked on the railroad as a fireman. The money he made was just enough to support the five children.

When Mr. Johnson was severely injured in an accident, he was no longer able to work. Mrs. Johnson took in washing and ironing to make money. Then, she worked as a cook at the YMCA. Johnson dropped out of school to help his mother. He babysat, ran errands, and worked in the fields.

In 1918, when he was seventeen years old, Johnson moved to New York City. He worked at a hotel, carrying bags and delivering food and messages. He worked as a cook, and he worked on the docks loading and unloading ships. Johnson sent money home and also set aside money for art school. It took him three years to save enough money to enroll in New York City's National Academy of Design (NAD).

The NAD taught an academic or traditional style of drawing and painting. Johnson did well there. He consistently won prizes for his work. During the summer, one of Johnson's instructors, Charles W. Hawthorne, ran the Cape Cod School of Art in Provincetown, Massachusetts. Johnson attended the summer program for three years. He worked as a maintenance man in exchange for room and board and tuition.

In his last year at the NAD, Johnson applied for the Pulitzer Traveling Scholarship. The $1,500 scholarship was awarded to "the most promising and deserving" student in an art school in the United States. Usually, the top student in the graduating class at the NAD won. Johnson was expected to win the award and was hurt when he did not win. Johnson's instructors felt that he had been unfairly overlooked because he was black. Charles Hawthorne contacted some friends and together they raised $1,000. That money was enough to send Johnson to Paris in November 1926.

Johnson experimented with new styles and new ways of using color in France. He also met Holcha Krake. Holcha was a weaver and ceramic artist from Denmark. Johnson spent the summer of 1929 traveling around Europe with Holcha, her sister Erna, and Erna's husband, the Expressionist painter Christophe Voll.

Johnson went back to New York in November. He entered six pieces in the Harmon Foundation's 1930 competition. Johnson won the Gold Medal and $400 prize for best painting. After the competition, he went to Florence to visit his family and exhibit his work at the YMCA.

■■■ *In this photograph, Johnson is shown painting a portrait.*

As Johnson was painting in front of the old Jacobai Hotel in Florence he was arrested. Johnson believed he was arrested because he was black. He left Florence to go to Denmark, where he married Holcha. They lived in a little fishing village called Kerteminde.

Johnson and Holcha traveled to the African country of Tunisia in the spring of 1932. They stayed in there for three months. When they returned home, they needed money. Johnson's work was not selling well. He wrote to Mary Brady of the Harmon Foundation and to Alain Locke, hoping they had sold some of his artwork. Locke had made no sales, and Brady had only sold two pieces. Johnson accused them of not working hard enough to sell his work. He explained his desperate need for cash but received only polite replies: the **Depression** made it hard for people to buy art.

In Europe, the Nazis condemned Expressionist art. Johnson's brother-in-law, Christophe Voll, lost his teaching job. Several artists were thrown into jail. Johnson and Holcha fled to the United States. Johnson looked for work for six months before he got a job with the WPA. He was assigned to teach art at the Harlem Community Center. While working in Harlem, he painted many neighborhood scenes. He exhibited work in two shows: the American Negro Exposition in Chicago and the New York's World Fair "Art of the WPA Projects."

The United States entered World War II on December 7, 1941. Thousands of black soldiers were sent overseas, and Johnson worked on a military series depicting their experiences. He also made several paintings about the Red Cross. Johnson received a certificate of honor for distinguished service to America in Art.

In 1942, a fire destroyed the Johnsons's apartment. In December 1943, Holcha was diagnosed with breast cancer. She died a few weeks later. Johnson returned to Florence to see his family. While there, he painted several family portraits.

Johnson decided to return to Denmark when the war was over. He got a job at a defense factory and started saving his money. Friends and family noticed that Johnson was not acting like himself. He did not bathe or shave regularly, and his behavior was unpredictable.

Despite his mental confusion, Johnson returned to Denmark in October of 1946. Johnson stayed with Holcha's family for several months and then went to Norway. He was found wandering the streets. The Norwegian police took him to a hospital, where he was diagnosed with a mental illness. He was sent back to the United States and transported to New York City's Central Islip State

Hospital in December 1947. When the Norwegian police found Johnson, he had $16,000 in his pocket. Boxes of his possessions and artwork surrounded him. The Norwegian government and Holcha's family made sure that Johnson's money and his possessions were returned to the United States. They tried to send these things to his mother, but she never received them.

A New York attorney was appointed Johnson's guardian. He stored Johnson's artwork in a warehouse until Johnson's money ran low. Then, he petitioned the court to have Johnson's artwork destroyed. In the meantime, he had Johnson's artwork appraised and valued at less than $100. The court granted permission to dispose of Johnson's work. The attorney gave Johnson's work to Mary Brady and the Harmon Foundation.

The Harmon Foundation arranged an exhibit, displaying over 1,500 pieces of Johnson's art. When the Foundation moved its New York office in 1967, Johnson's work moved to the National Collection of Fine Arts, which is now called the National Museum of American Art. The Foundation also gave pieces to black colleges, the Oakland Museum, and the Library of Congress.

William Henry Johnson never left the hospital. He died on April 13, 1970. The respect and recognition that he had longed for was his, but he was not able to enjoy it.

▮▮ *Jim*, by William H. Johnson (c. 1930)
Many of Johnson's portraits used dark colors and showed the subject against a plain background in order to focus on the person's feelings.

Lois Mailou Jones (1905–1998)

- Born November 3, 1905, in Boston, Massachusetts
- Died June 9, 1998, in Washington, D.C.

Key works
Negro Cabin, Sedalia, North Carolina, 1930
The Ascent of Ethiopia, 1932
Les Fetiches, 1938

When Lois Mailou Jones was offered a scholarship to the Designers Art School of Boston, she was pleased. Jones, a gifted young artist, had just graduated from Boston's High School of Practical Arts. Art school was the next obvious step.

Jones did not expect to have to do maid service. The scholarship would be granted only if she agreed to clean the studio every day. Jones thought about refusing the scholarship, but her mother convinced her to take it.

Mrs. Jones agreed to do the cleaning. That way, Jones could get the scholarship and not be embarrassed. "She did it at a great sacrifice for me," Jones later recalled.

Lois Mailou Jones was born on November 3, 1905, in Boston, Massachusetts, to Thomas and Carolyn Adams Jones. The Jones family lived in an apartment on the top floor of an office building. Mr. Jones was the maintenance man for the building.

Mrs. Jones was a beautician. She had many wealthy white **patrons**. She often took Jones with her when she went to do their hair. Jones saw lots of beautiful paintings in their homes. The paintings she saw inspired her to draw.

Jones went to the Boston High School of Practical Arts. A counselor at the school helped Jones apply to the art school of Boston's Museum of Fine Arts. When school was out at 2:00 P.M., Jones worked in the museum school until about 4:30. She also worked at the museum on Saturdays.

Jones was able to see the art in the museum every day. She learned a lot listening to art instructors and museum **curators** discuss the particulars of the different types of design and different artists' work.

Jones also learned about art from Meta Vaux Warrick Fuller, a well-known sculptor. Jones was a teenager when she met Fuller. They worked together on costumes for a play at a black community center.

Jones and Fuller met again when they spent summers on Martha's Vineyard, an island in New England. Jones's family owned a house there. Fuller also vacationed on Martha's Vineyard. The two women became good friends. Fuller encouraged Jones to become an artist.

Jones accepted a scholarship to the Designers Art School of Boston when she finished high school. When Jones graduated, she tried to market her designs for fabrics, but her race was a problem. Most textile houses would not give her the opportunity to show her designs.

A white friend from school helped her. When this friend took her own designs to textile houses, she also took one or two of Jones's designs with her. If the textile house liked Jones's designs, they bought them. Later, they found out who had designed the work.

Jones applied for a position at the Museum of Fine Arts as an assistant teacher. Her interviewer told her there were no positions available but asked her if she had ever thought of going south to teach.

■■ *This photograph of Lois Mailou Jones was taken during the Harlem Renaissance.*

Meta Vaux Warrick Fuller (1877–1968)

Meta Vaux Warrick Fuller was a well-known African-American sculptor. Her career began long before the Harlem Renaissance took place and continued long after it ended. Fuller was one of the first artists to focus on African-American experiences as subjects of her work.

Fuller was born in Philadelphia, Pennsylvania. She attended the Pennsylvania School of Industrial Arts and the Colarossi Academy in Paris, France. While in Paris, Fuller studied with Auguste Rodin, a famous French sculptor.

Jones moved to North Carolina and started an art department at a black high school. Two years later, Jones was asked to start an art department at Howard University, in Washington, D.C. Jones went to Howard University in 1930. She taught design, drawing, and watercolor.

Jones's teaching schedule kept her busy. In 1937, she took a year off and traveled to Paris. She enrolled in the Academie Julien. Jones spent the year in Paris creating paintings in the **Impressionist** tradition. Her landscapes received good reviews when Parisian art galleries displayed them.

In 1934, Jones took a design class at Columbia University in New York. She met an African dancer, Asadata Dafora. Jones designed some masks for Dafora's dance company and helped with costume design. She also met a young Haitian artist named Louis Vergniaud Pierre-Noel around this time.

In 1938, Jones painted *Les Fetiches*, the first of several pictures with African masks as the subject matter. *Les Fetiches* attracted the attention of Alain Locke. Locke encouraged Jones to consider African Americans as subject matter. She followed his advice. Jones traveled to France every summer to paint. However, her African-American heritage became more evident in her work.

In 1953, Jones married Vergniaud Pierre-Noel, the Haitian artist she had met years earlier in New York. They moved to Haiti. In Haiti, Jones studied the art and culture of the Haitian people. Her painting and design became more colorful and more **abstract**. While in Haiti, Jones taught watercolor and painting. She painted portraits of the Haitian president and his wife. The president of Haiti gave her a national award for her teaching and paintings.

After a trip to Africa in 1971, more African artifacts and designs showed up in Jones's work. Jones felt that she had "a clearer picture of the various ways in which African art has influenced the work of the Afro-American artist."

Jones was honored for her achievements as an artist in 1972. The Museum of the National Center of Afro-American Artists and the Boston Museum of Fine Art hosted an exhibition of Jones's work. In 1980, she was invited to the White House, where President Jimmy Carter recognized the works of ten African-American artists.

Over the years, Jones won numerous awards for her art. However, she is best known as a teacher and motivator of young artists. She taught at Howard University for 47 years, retiring in 1977.

Lois Mailou Jones died in Washington, D.C., on June 9, 1998. In 1999, the Mint Museum of Art in Charlotte, North Carolina, celebrated Jones's teaching and her talent by hosting an exhibition called "Lois Mailou Jones and Her Former Students: An American Legacy."

The Ascent of Ethiopia, by Lois Mailou Jones (1932)
This painting shows Jones's interest in African themes.

Archibald J. Motley Jr. (1891–1981)

- Born October 7, 1891, in New Orleans, Louisiana
- Died January 16, 1981, in Chicago, Illinois

Key works
Blues, 1929
The Jockey Club, 1929
Saturday Night Street Scene, 1936

"Don't enter that painting," the president of the African-American Chicago Art League advised Motley. He was sure the painting would be rejected from the art competition. More importantly, he was afraid the painting would reinforce stereotypes about African Americans. Motley disagreed. He entered his painting and won the competition. *Syncopation,* a painting depicting an African-American dance hall scene, won the Joseph Eisendrath Award and $200.

"[Black artists] were awfully afraid, years ago, of sending anything that was **Negroid** to any of the exhibitions," Motley later recalled. "Well, I myself, felt they belonged..." Motley became well known for his colorful images of the African-American social scene.

Archibald J. Motley, Jr. was born October 7, 1891, to Archibald Motley, Sr. and Mary Huff in New Orleans, Louisiana. Mr. Motley owned a general store. One day, some white men came and threatened Mr. Motley. His store was taking business away from white storeowners. If Mr. Motley valued his life, he should find somewhere else to do business. Mr. Motley packed up his family and left town. The Motleys moved to Chicago. Mr. Motley found work as a porter in the Pullman cars.

Motley was always drawing. His school notebooks were filled with sketches. He wanted to be an artist when he grew up, but his father disagreed. Mr. Motley did not think art was a practical career.

Mr. Motley worked in the train's buffet car. One of the regular riders, Dr. Frank Gunasulus, was the head of an Illinois college, the Armour Institute. He heard Mr. Motley talking about his talented son and asked to meet him. The young Motley impressed Gunasulus, and he offered him a **scholarship** to study architecture at Armour. Motley turned it down. He did not want to be an architect; he wanted to be an artist.

Motley's desire to be an artist impressed Gunasulus even more. He offered to pay for Motley's first year at the School of the Art Institute of Chicago. Motley accepted his offer.

Motley earned enough money to pay for the next three years at the Art Institute himself. He worked part-time cleaning and doing odd jobs. His father gave him 25 cents a day. Motley spent one summer working as a porter on the train. He traveled the country and sketched wherever the train stopped. He also started painting. Canvas was expensive, and Motley could not afford it. He took old laundry bags and used them instead of canvas.

Motley graduated from the School of the Art Institute of Chicago in 1918. He looked for work as a commercial artist but could not find it. Motley took a number of hard, dirty jobs to earn money. In his free time, he painted.

In 1919, Motley attended lectures by the American painter George Bellows at the Art Institute of Chicago. Bellows painted ordinary people enjoying life. He gave his subjects dignity. Motley, too, believed in the value of portraying people in normal activities. Bellows's work helped Motley to think seriously about moving in another direction.

Motley was afraid to enter his work in art shows. In 1921, a friend talked Motley into entering the Art Institute's annual art show. Motley's piece did not win a prize, but it did receive favorable comments. Motley was encouraged to enter other shows.

In 1924, Motley married Edith Granzo, a German girl who lived across the street from him. They experienced racism and discrimination because of their **interracial** marriage.

Archiabld J. Motley was both an artist and an activist for promoting African–American art. He served as the director of the Chicago No-Jury Society and fought to have more African Americans included in art shows.

In 1925, Motley submitted *Mending Socks,* a portrait of his grandmother, for competition. The portrait received good reviews. Then, two pieces took the top prize in two separate competitions —*Syncopation* received the Joseph Eisendrath Award and *A Mulatress* won the $200 Frank G. Logan Prize. Motley's work attracted the attention of French art critic, Count Chabrier. Chabrier wrote two articles about Motley and praised his work. When the articles appeared in Parisian art magazines, critics paid more attention to Motley's work.

Around this time, Motley was elected director of the Chicago No-Jury Society of Art. He was the first African American to hold this position. Robert B. Harsche, director of the Art Institute of Chicago, helped Motley get into two shows: Painting and Watercolors by Living American Artists in 1927 and the Harmon Foundation Awards for Distinguished Achievement Among Negroes in 1928. *Mending Socks* won the "most popular" prize in the Painting and Watercolors by Living American Artists show and *The Old Snuff Dipper* won the Harmon gold medal in 1928.

Harsche contacted important New York galleries to arrange an exhibition of Motley's paintings. His work paid off. Motley opened a one-man show at New Galleries in New York City. Good reviews and an article about Motley in the *New York Times* encouraged people to see the exhibit. Once they saw the work, they wanted it. Motley sold most of the paintings in the exhibition. In 1929, Motley won a Guggenheim **Fellowship,** an award that allowed him to study in Europe for one year. Unlike many artists who studied in Paris, Motley's style did not change significantly when he returned to the United States in 1930.

Soon after he returned to the United States, the Great **Depression** began. People had little money to spend on art, and jobs were scarce. Motley found work as a supervisor with the WPA Federal Art Project. He earned enough to support himself; Edith; and their son, Archibald Motley III, who was born in 1931. Motley gave up his WPA position temporarily in 1935, when he won a design competition for the U.S. Postal Service.

The U.S. Postal Service sent Motley to Wood River, a small town in southern Illinois, to paint a mural on the wall in the post office. People stared at him as he walked around town. He was later told that there were no black people in Wood River, and the people were curious about him.

In 1945, Edith died. Motley became severely depressed and was unable to work. Later, he found a job in a factory that painted designs on plastic shower curtains. Motley painted according to instructions, filling in color between black lines.

Eight years later, Motley was still working at the curtain factory. His nephew, Willard Motley, a wealthy novelist, hoped that a change of scenery would help his uncle recover from his depression. In 1953, Willard invited Motley to visit his home in Cuernavaca, Mexico.

The long visit at Willard's home reawakened Motley's desire to paint. He painted twelve pictures during his Mexican visit. Motley continued to paint and celebrate African-American life through the 1960s and 1970s. Young black artists criticized Motley for not addressing contemporary social problems. He was hurt by the criticism, but he did not let it affect his work.

In 1972, the National Conference of Artists recognized Motley for his contribution to art. In 1980, he was one of ten artists to be honored by President Jimmy Carter. Motley died in Chicago on January 16, 1981. His artwork celebrated the social aspects of the African-American experience. Motley, very much a part of the New Negro movement, proved that the Renaissance was not limited to Harlem.

■■■ *Mending Socks,* by Motley (1924)
This painting of Motley's grandmother was popular with the public.

Augusta Savage (1892–1962)

- Born February 29, 1892, in Green Cove Springs, Florida
- Died March 27, 1962, in New York, New York

Key works
Gamin, 1930
La Citadelle—Freedom, 1930
Lift Every Voice and Sing, 1939

Augusta Savage gathered clay from the brickyards and pinched and poked until an image formed. Her father was not pleased. He whipped her whenever he caught her modeling. "My father licked me five or six times a week," Savage later recalled. "[He] almost licked all the art out of me." Poverty and racism finally licked the art out of Savage. After years of struggle, she gave up; she just quit working.

Augusta Savage was born in Green Cove Springs, Florida, on February 29, 1892, to Edward and Cornelia Fells. Augusta was the seventh of fourteen children. The main industry in Green Cove Springs was bricks. Several clay pits were located nearby because clay was important to brick making. Savage taught herself to model in the clay pits.

When Savage was about fifteen years old, her family moved to West Palm Beach, Florida. Savage made friends with the local potter, who gave her modeling clay. During her senior year of high school, Savage taught a modeling class to her peers.

In 1907, Savage married John T. Moore. Moore died unexpectedly, leaving Savage with a baby to support. She moved back to her parents' home and tried to figure out what to do.

She decided to sell some of her figurines at the county fair. She earned $175 and won a $25 prize for the most original booth. The fair superintendent commissioned Savage to make a portrait of him. Then, he encouraged her to go to New York to study sculpture. He wrote to a well-known New York sculptor, Solon Borglum, and asked him to help her.

Savage went to New York, but she did not study with Borglum. His fees were too expensive. He suggested that she go to Cooper Union, a famous New York art school that gave free classes. Savage started Cooper Union's four-year sculpture program in October 1921. While in New York, Savage met a carpenter named James Savage. The couple married, then divorced a few months later. After her divorce, she kept the name Augusta Savage.

Savage's skills were so advanced that she completed the first two years course work in six weeks. She was working on third year work when she ran out of money. She explained the situation to Kate Reynolds, the school registrar. Reynolds convinced the Cooper Union Advisory Council to give Savage a special scholarship that covered living and traveling expenses. She was able to stay and complete the program.

In 1923, the French government sponsored a summer art program for women

in Fountainebleau, France. Savage applied for admission to the program, but her application was rejected. She got angry when she learned who was selected. She knew her work was much better than some of those chosen to go to Fountainebleau. Savage believed she was excluded because she was black.

She complained to the Ethical Culture Committee. She wrote letters to newspapers. Other people joined Savage's attempt to get the Fountainebleau committee to reverse its decision. They were unsuccessful.

▌▌▌ *Augusta Savage was an artist and a teacher. Her work for the Harlem Community Art Center inspired a new generation of black artists.*

Savage was labeled a troublemaker. The artists, curators, and administrators that served on the Fountainebleau committee worked on other committees or in museums and art galleries. As a result, Savage had difficulty getting her pieces exhibited.

Savage was **commissioned** to make a bust of editor and civil rights activist W.E.B. Du Bois for the Harlem branch of the New York Public Library. Her next commission was for a portrait of Marcus Garvey, another black leader. While working on Garvey's bust, Savage met and married his secretary-general, Robert L. Poston. This marriage did not last long either. Poston died on his way home from a business trip less than a year after their wedding.

In 1925, Savage was offered a scholarship to the Royal Academy of Fine Arts in Rome. The scholarship covered tuition and art materials; it did not cover travel or living expenses. Savage, unable to raise enough money to meet the additional expenses, could not accept the scholarship.

Savage created *Gamin* in 1929. This bust of a young boy attracted the attention of two prominent Harlem businessmen. The men asked administrators of the Julius Rosenwald Fund to help Savage by offering her a fellowship. After having her work evaluated by experts, they awarded Savage two fellowships for study abroad.

This time, Savage made it to Europe. The African-American community in New York had learned of Savage's struggles with Fountainebleau and the Roman Scholarship. People took up collections, held fund-raising parties, and donated the money to Savage. Bit by bit, the community raised enough money to send Savage to Europe and pay for living expenses once she got there.

Savage enrolled in the Academie de la Grande Chaumiere in Paris, France. She stayed in Paris for two years. When she returned to the New York, the Great **Depression** had begun. Savage showed her work at several galleries, but few people were buying art.

In 1934, she produced the bust of a handicapped musician. Based on this piece, Savage was the first African-American woman elected to the National Association of Women Painters and Sculptors. In 1939, she was commissioned to do a bust of writer and civil rights leader, James Weldon Johnson. She received other commissions but not enough to make a living.

The Harlem Community Arts Center started in Savage's studio. It began as the Savage Studio of Arts and Crafts. Savage started teaching a few children, but the numbers grew. Eventually, she applied for a grant from the Carnegie

Foundation, because she could not manage the students and supplies alone. When the WPA Federal Art Project started, Savage received more assistance, and her studio became known as the Harlem Community Arts Center.

The WPA organized art projects to assist artists during the Depression. However, the WPA hired few black artists. Savage argued with WPA administrators to employ black artists. She also helped form the Harlem Artists Guild and the Vanguard Club to address problems unique to black artists. People accused the Vanguard Club of being a **communist** organization. Political pressure forced the Harlem Community Arts Center to close.

Savage was commissioned to do a large piece representing "the American Negro's contribution to music" for the 1939 New York World's Fair. She created *Lift Every Voice and Sing.* This sculpture was over sixteen feet tall. Savage could not afford to have it cast. When the buildings for the fair were torn down, the sculpture was destroyed.

Later that year, Savage planned to show her work at the American Negro Exposition in Chicago. She took a number of pieces with her to show in the exhibition. The only piece Savage showed at the Exhibition was *Prima Donna.* She did not win any prizes. Disappointed and depressed, Savage returned to New York. Somewhere along the way, much of her work disappeared.

Savage gave up on art. She moved to an old chicken farm in Saugerties, New York. She had nothing to do with art or artists. She died March 27, 1962, in a hospital in New York City.

Most of Augusta Savage's works have disappeared or been destroyed. They are only visible in photographs. Despite this, Savage inspired a generation of young artists. She is considered one of the most influential artists of the Harlem Renaissance.

■■ *La Citadelle—Freedom,* by Augusta Savage (1930)
   Savage fought against discrimination her entire life.
   The idea of freedom was important to her.

James Van Der Zee (1886–1983)

- Born June 29, 1886, in Lenox, Massachusetts
- Died May 15, 1983, in New York, New York

Key works

Victory Parade of 369 Regiment, 1919
Dancer, Harlem, 1925
Portrait Of Couple With Raccoon Coats and Stylish Car, 1932

James Van Der Zee eagerly tore open the package. He took out a small box of glass plates, several chemical packets, and finally, a box camera. He peered through the tiny lens. How on earth was he going to take pictures with this? Van Der Zee never learned to use that camera. However, he did learn to use other cameras. He became one of the best photographers of his day. Van Der Zee captured the mood, people, and places of Harlem. He was known as Harlem's "picture-taking man."

James Van Der Zee was born June 29, 1886, in Lenox, Massachusetts, to John and Susan Van Der Zee. He was the second of six children. Van Der Zee attended the public schools in his neighborhood. Often, he and his brothers and sisters were the only black children in their classes. Winter evenings, the Van Der Zee family gathered in the parlor playing instruments or singing, drawing, or painting. Van Der Zee played the piano and the violin. He enjoyed the music, but drawing and painting bored him.

"One day, I saw a little advertisement ... that said I could get a camera and outfit for selling so many packages of sachet, and I knew that was a way I could get rid of all this drawing and painting," said Van Der Zee.

He ordered the sachet packages and worked hard to sell them when they came in the mail. When he sold all his goods, he mailed the money to the company and waited for the camera. Van Der Zee was disappointed when the camera came. He studied the instructions carefully, but he was not able to make a single picture. The camera was too primitive. So Van Der Zee got a job helping a lady plant her garden. She paid him 25 cents an hour. He worked long enough to save five dollars. Then, he bought a camera that worked.

The new camera did not come with a roll of film. Van Der Zee had to use glass plates and powders for picture taking. He also had to develop the photographs himself. He bought chemicals from a store and set up a darkroom in his bedroom closet. When the prints were made, he laid them in the sun to dry.

He practiced taking pictures of his family, neighbors, and friends. One day, a teacher saw him photographing classmates and asked how much he would charge for prints. "Ten cents apiece," Van Der Zee replied. Soon he was selling photographs to his teacher, schoolmates, and neighbors.

In 1906, the twenty-year-old Van Der Zee moved to New York City. He worked as a waiter and elevator operator. He took some music classes and joined two musical clubs. Then, he joined a band.

While playing at St. Mark's church in New York City, Van Der Zee met Kate Brown. They were married in March of 1907. When Kate became pregnant, the Van Der Zees moved to Phoebus, Virginia, to be closer to Kate's family. Van Der Zee worked at the Hotel Chamberlain. In his spare time, he photographed people in their natural environment. He photographed children at school, blacksmiths in their shops, and people on porches. He also spent a lot of time photographing his daughter, Rachel, who was born on September 22, 1907.

Van Der Zee and Kate moved back to Harlem in the spring of 1908. He took more music classes, and he formed the Harlem Orchestra. He continued to do odd jobs and gave private lessons to earn money.

During this period, the Van Der Zees had another child, a son named Emil. Unfortunately, Emil caught pneumonia and died when he was a year old. The baby's death strained the marriage. Kate began to take long trips home to visit her family. Van Der Zee stayed in New York.

▮▮ *Self-Portrait* by James Van Der Zee (1931)
Van Der Zee was a self-taught photographer who left a large collection of photographs—a record of life in Harlem during the Harlem Renaissance.

Phonographs and jukeboxes became popular, and Van Der Zee's music business failed. People were buying records instead of hiring bands to play at their parties. Worried about making a living, Van Der Zee thought, "... I might look into photographing again."

Van Der Zee found work at a small camera shop in Newark, New Jersey. He developed film and, if the photographer/shop owner was not available, he took photographs. Van Der Zee worked carefully with the subjects. He posed them different ways and retouched the photographs to make the subjects look their best. Soon, people were coming in just to have Van Der Zee make their portraits. He was generating a lot of business, but the shop owner did not offer him a raise.

Van Der Zee left the camera shop and returned to Harlem. He went into a partnership with his sister and brother-in-law. He opened a studio in connection with the music school they operated. He attracted attention by putting unusual props and photos in the window. People walking by were intrigued by the display and dropped in. Soon, Van Der Zee was photographing all kinds of people: soldiers, families, businessmen, politicians, and celebrities.

Van Der Zee became dissatisfied with the arrangement. He brought in a lot of money, but his partners were getting most of it. They paid him a weekly salary. Meanwhile, Kate had left him and filed for a divorce. Van Der Zee decided it was time to work independently.

Van Der Zee named his first studio Guarantee Photo Studio. When he moved to another location sometime later, he renamed the business GGG Photo. Van Der Zee married Gaynella Greenlee in 1916. If he was not in the shop when someone needed a picture made, Gaynella would send one of the neighborhood boys to find him.

One day, Van Der Zee was at the barbershop getting a hair cut when a boy ran in. "Is the picture-takin' man here?" the boy asked. He said Van Der Zee was needed over at the "picture-takin' place." After that, Van Der Zee was known all over Harlem as the "picture-takin' man."

Van Der Zee specialized in photographing families, church groups, and social organizations. He went into people's homes, and he photographed people on the street. He went to pool halls, bus stations, school playgrounds, and barbershops. Over the next 30 years, Van Der Zee provided a photo documentary of Harlem's people and their lives.

When Polaroid and Kodak camera companies came out with inexpensive, easy-to-use cameras in the 1940s and 1950s, Van Der Zee's business declined. He moved into photo restoration, but this did not pay well.

In 1969, the Metropolitan Museum of Art produced an exhibit called "Harlem on My Mind." Van Der Zee was a major contributor. He offered the largest and most complete photo documentation of Harlem. The exhibition renewed interest in Van Der Zee's work. He was granted an honorary degree and given several awards.

However, all was not well. Van Der Zee had been evicted from his studio. He was living in poverty. People had stolen some of his priceless negatives and photographs. In 1969, friends helped form the James Van Der Zee Institute to house his large collection of negatives and photographs. Gaynella Greenlee died in 1976. In 1978, the 92-year-old Van Der Zee married Donna Mussaden.

In 1981, Van Der Zee sued the Studio Museum of Harlem. He wanted possession of the 125,000 negatives and prints in the James Van Der Zee Institute that had become a part of the Studio Museum of Harlem. Van Der Zee said he had received little compensation for his materials. When the lawsuit was filed, the collection was valued at over ten million dollars.

The "picture-taking man" died May 14, 1984. He is remembered as an innovator who documented Harlem's history.

In this photograph, Van Der Zee shows two veterans of World War I. Many African-American soldiers fought in the war. Some Harlem Renaissance artists, such as Palmer Hayden, served in the military during the war.

Hale Aspacio Woodruff (1900–1980)

- Born August 26, 1900, in Cairo, Illinois
- Died September 26, 1980, in New York, New York

Key works
The Banjo Player, 1927
Paris Landscape, 1927
Chartres, 1928
Amistad Mutiny Murals, 1938–1939
The Art of the Negro, 1951

"I was an only child... there were times when I found myself by myself. So I'd just sit down and draw. My mother was very, very skillful . . . in drawing, and I soon found a satisfaction in this very exciting way to pass the time. So in a way, you might say I made a career out of a hobby that I developed early in life," said Hale Woodruff.

Woodruff was an important influence on the next generation of African-American artists. He was a popular artist and teacher.

Woodruff's career spanned over 50 years. He was one of the best painters, muralists, and art teachers of his day. He was born August 26, 1900, in Cairo, Illinois, to George and Augusta Woodruff. George Woodruff died soon after his son's birth. Augusta went to Nashville, Tennessee, where she worked as a maid.

When Woodruff was older, his mother often left him alone when she went to work. He entertained himself by drawing pictures. When he started school, he copied pictures from his schoolbooks. Mrs. Woodruff worked hard, but there was never enough money. When Woodruff was twelve years old, he got a job at Holt's Café. Woodruff gave the money to his mother.

Woodruff drew cartoons for his high school newspaper, The *Pearl High Voice.* He spent time in the school library reading *Crisis* magazine. *Crisis* featured illustrations by black artists, and articles and news about black artists. One of these artists was Henry O. Tanner. Woodruff vowed that one day he would go to Europe and meet Tanner.

In the summer of 1918, Woodruff graduated from Pearl High School. He went to Indianapolis, Indiana, to look for work and plan for college. He rented a room at the YMCA on Senate Avenue and found work at a hotel scrubbing floors and cleaning carpets. In 1920, he enrolled in the John Herron Art Institute in Indianapolis.

The art school's tuition had to be paid in advance. His mother sent what money she could, but Woodruff needed more. The YMCA gave him a job as desk clerk in exchange for his room and board. He worked in a restaurant washing dishes, and he earned money drawing cartoons for a black weekly newspaper, *The Indianapolis Ledger.* Eventually, Woodruff could not pay the year's tuition in advance. He had to drop out of school. He moved to Chicago, hoping to find a job that paid more. He applied to the School of the Art Institute in Chicago.

Woodruff was admitted to the School of the Art Institute, but he did not like it. He returned to Indianapolis and to his job at the YMCA. He painted in his spare time, and he began to experiment with landscapes. One day, a friend gave him the book *African Sculpture* by Carl Einstein. Woodruff later recalled:

> You can't imagine the effect that book had on me. Part of the effect was due to the fact that as a black artist I felt very much alone there in Indianapolis. I had heard of Tanner, but I had never heard of the significance of the impact of African art. Yet here it was! ...Sculptures of black people, my people, they were considered very beautiful by these German art experts! The whole idea that this could be so was like an explosion. It was a real turning point for me.

Soon, Woodruff was exhibiting his work in art shows at the Indiana State Fair, the Indianapolis Museum, and the Herron Museum. The Senate Avenue YMCA was a cultural center for the African-American community as well as a home for young men. The YMCA director brought in national speakers on cultural, political, and social issues relevant to African Americans. He also held art shows and exhibits; Woodruff exhibited his work in those shows, too.

In 1926, Woodruff entered five paintings in the Harmon Foundation's competition for Distinguished Achievement Among Negroes. He won second place and a $100 cash prize. The local newspapers wrote articles about him, and the governor of Indiana presented him with a medal.

Woodruff wanted to study in Paris, but he could not afford it. A women's group put on a play and raised $200 for his Paris trip. He sold several paintings, and soon, he had enough money to finance his trip. On September 3, 1927, the 27-year-old

Woodruff sailed for France. Woodruff enrolled in the Academie Moderne and the Academie Scandinave. While in France, he remembered his dream to meet Henry O. Tanner. He wrote to Tanner and asked if he could come visit. Tanner did not reply. Woodruff decided to just drop in. He went to the village where Tanner lived and knocked on the door. Tanner welcomed Woodruff. They had a long talk about art and black artists.

After two years in France, Woodruff was out of money. He had no money to pay expenses or to buy food. He was starving. He applied to the Rosenwald Fund for a **fellowship** but was turned down. One day, he stopped by the American Express office to pick up his mail and was surprised to find a $200 check waiting for him. The Harmon Foundation had sold one of his paintings.

Woodruff stayed in France for four years because he did not have enough money to go home. He had trouble finding work because he was not a French citizen. Determined to find a job, Woodruff pretended to be a French citizen from North Africa. He got a job on a road-gang moving rocks. In 1931, Woodruff left France to start an art department at Atlanta University.

Chartres, by Hale Woodruff (1928)
This was painted during Woodruff's years in France. He was influenced by modern painters in France and also learned a lot from Henry O. Tanner.

The art department consisted of two rooms in a basement. Woodruff taught art appreciation, drawing, and painting. He encouraged his students to look at their community and paint what they saw. He took them to museums and showed them different styles of art. He arranged for traveling art shows to come to Atlanta, and he held student art exhibitions.

In 1934, Woodruff married Theresa Baker. Soon after his marriage, Woodruff received a grant to go to Mexico to study Mexican art. Woodruff worked with Diego Rivera, a famous painter and muralist. Rivera put Woodruff to work mixing colors and preparing walls for a mural project on the Hotel Reforma in Mexico City. When the mural was finished, Woodruff worked with other Mexican painters. He went back to the United States with a broader perspective on color and ideas for murals of his own. Woodruff painted murals at the Atlanta School of Social Work after returning from Mexico. In 1939, he completed the Amistad murals for Talladega College in Alabama.

The Harmon Foundation had stopped its annual negro art exhibitions in 1935. Woodruff convinced officials at Atlanta University to take over this role. The Atlanta University Annual Exhibition opened on April 29, 1942. The exhibition went well and the reviews were good.

Woodruff received a Rosenwald Fellowship in 1943 and 1944. He took a leave of absence from Atlanta University and went to New York to study. During this period, Woodruff began to experiment with abstract art. Woodruff 's work impressed New York critics. He was asked to teach at New York University. He would make more money and have greater social freedom in New York than in the segregated South. By this time, Woodruff had a son named Roy. After thinking things over, Woodruff accepted the position and moved his family to New York in 1946.

In 1948, Woodruff and another black muralist, Charles Alston, painted a mural depicting the history of blacks in California for the Golden State Mutual Life Insurance Company. Three years later, Woodruff completed a mural titled *The Art of the Negro* for Atlanta University.

In 1962, Woodruff helped found Spiral, an organization of black artists. In 1966, his students named him "Great Teacher." In 1968, he retired from teaching. Hale Woodruff died in New York on September 26, 1980. Many mourned the 80-year-old painter. Major art museums and many African-American colleges and universities still exhibit Woodruff's work.

The Next Generation

The Harlem Renaissance was a brief period in the history of American Art. However, its effects were profound. African-American artists proved that with hope, talent, and persistence, African-American art could and would be brought to the public.

Many artists involved in the Harlem Renaissance were teachers. Artists like Augusta Savage, Lois Mailou Jones, and Hale Aspacio Woodruff taught the art they loved to younger artists. They also influenced the work of artists who came after them.

Charles H. Alston

Charles H. Alston was born November 28, 1907, in Charlotte, North Carolina. Alston earned a fine arts degree from Columbia University in 1925, then went to Columbia's Teachers College to earn a master's degree.

African art forms had a big influence on Alston's artistic development. Africa's influence is obvious in many of his murals and sculpture. Alston's best known works include the Golden State Life Insurance Company murals and a bronze sculpture portrait of Dr. Martin Luther King, Jr. From 1948 to 1949, he worked with Hale Woodruff on a series of murals in California.

Alston taught art at New York City's Art Students League and City College. He died of cancer in 1977.

Romare Bearden

Romare Bearden is best known for his use of collage. A collage is a two-dimensional work of cut, torn, and pasted papers.

Romare Bearden was born September 2, 1914, in Charlotte, North Carolina. He graduated from New York University with a degree in mathematics. Bearden quickly discovered that he did not want to teach math. He wanted to be an artist. He took a drawing class at Augusta Savage's art school in Harlem. He enjoyed that class, so he enrolled in the Art Students League in New York and then studied in Paris.

▮▮ *The Female Worker...* by Jacob Lawrence (1940–1941)
Lawrence painted stories of African-American life. This painting is part of a series of paintings about the great migration.

Romare Bearden saw African-American people move from a rural to an urban lifestyle. He recorded that change in his art. Some of Bearden's pieces show people working in fields. Other pieces show crowded city streets, apartment houses, and nightclub scenes. Romare Bearden's work is a record of African-American life. Toward the end of his life, Bearden served as a historian of the Harlem Renaissance. He died in 1988.

Jacob Lawrence

Jacob Lawrence was born September 7, 1917, in Atlantic City, New Jersey. His family moved to Harlem, New York, in 1930. Lawrence taught himself to paint. He worked with Charles Alston at the neighborhood art center briefly, and he met Augusta Savage at a WPA art program.

Lawrence's work tells a story. He painted the migration of African Americans from the South to the North. He painted the Haitian hero, Toussaint L'Ouverture, and the heroic deeds of Harriet Tubman. He also illustrated a book of poetry by Langston Hughes.

Jacob Lawrence taught art at various schools and universities from 1955 to 1983. In 1998, Lawrence was diagnosed with lung cancer. He died at his home in Seattle, Washington, on June 9, 2000.

Black Manhattan by Romare Bearden (1969)
In this work, Bearden created a collage of photographs to show what life was like in New York City.

55

Timeline

1886   James Van Der Zee born June 29

1887   Sargent Claude Johnson born October 7

1890   Palmer Hayden born January 15

1891   Archibald J. Motley, Jr. born October 7

1892   Augusta Savage born February 29

1896   Malvin Gray Johnson born January 2

1900   Hale Aspacio Woodruff born August 26

1901   Richmond Barthe born January 28
       William H. Johnson born March 18

1905   Lois Mailou Jones born November 3

1907   Charles H. Alston born November 28

1909   National Association for the Advancement of Colored People (NAACP) founded

1914   World War I begins n Europe

1917   United States enters World War I

1919   World War I ends

1920   Palmer Hayden leaves military; goes to New York to study art at Cooper Union

1921   William H. Johnson enrolls in the National Academy of Design

1923   *Opportunity*, the official journal of the Urban League, is published

1924   Aaron Douglas moves to New York City, begins studying with Winold Reiss

1926   The Harmon Foundation holds the first annual competition and exhibition of artwork submitted for "Distinguished Achievement Among Negroes"

1929   Stock market crashes

1930 Lois Mailou Jones accepts teaching position at Howard University

1931 Hale Woodruff accepts teaching position at Atlanta University

1933 Harlem Community Art Center opened, managed by Augusta Savage
WPA (Works Progress Administration) Federal Arts Project begins

1934 Malvin Gray Johnson dies October 4

1935 The last Harmon Foundation competition held

1937 Aaron Douglas begins teaching at Fisk University

1939 World War II begins in Europe

1941 United States enters Word War II

1945 World War II ends

1947 William H. Johnson hospitalized in the Central Islip State Hospital

1962 Augusta Savage dies on March 27

1963 W.E.B. Du Bois dies

1967 Sargent Claude Johnson dies

1969 "Harlem On My Mind" exhibition opens at the Metropolitan Museum of Art

1970 William H. Johnson dies

1973 Palmer Hayden dies

1979 Aaron Douglas dies

1980 Ten African-American artists honored by President Jimmy Carter

1981 Archibald J. Motley dies

1984 James Van Der Zee dies

1989 Richmond Barthe dies on March 5

Glossary

abstract art art that emphasizes bold color or design, giving the artist's impression of an object instead of showing the object in a realistic manner, so that the subject may or may not be identifiable

academic art that is created using ideas about line and color that date back to the 1400s and that always represents an object or person in a realistic way

Abstract Expressionism artistic movement based in New York City in the 1950s, made up of artists who painted their emotions using bold color and line; an artist who was active in Abstract Expressionism is called an Abstract Expressionist

bust sculpture of a person's head and shoulders

cast metal copy of a piece of art created by pouring a liquid metal into a mold and letting it harden; or the act of pouring liquid-metal into a mold to create a metal copy

cavalry soldiers in the army who fight on horseback

commission to place an order for a work of art, or to ask an artist to create a piece of art for a fee

communist person who believes that people should not have their own possessions, but that all of the people in a country should own all goods collectively and should share them equally

composition arrangement of the parts or elements of a piece of art, such as the line, shape, and color

Cubism artistic movement based in Paris in the early 1900s, made up of artists interested in painting or sculpting a subject in geometric shapes like squares and triangles; an artist who was active in Cubism is called a Cubist

curator person who conducts research and selects artwork for a museum or art gallery

depression time when there is not a lot of business development taking place in a country, and many people are unemployed

Expressionism artistic movement based in Germany in the early 1900s, made up of artists interested in using color, lighting, and symbolism to show a strong mood or feeling; an artist who was active in Expressionism is called an Expressionist

fellowship money awarded to a student to pursue a course of study

Impressionism artistic movement based in France in the 1870s, made up of artists interested in using light and color to depict their impression of a subject at a certain moment; an artist who was active in Impressionism is called an Impressionist

interracial describes something that is shared between two races; a marriage of a black person and a white person is called an interracial marriage

lithograph kind of print made when an artist draws an image on a smooth stone that is used to create many copies of the image on paper

Modernism style of art that emphasizes breaking away from the traditions of the past and exploring new forms of art

monochromatic artwork made using a single color and its various tints and shades instead of many colors

patron someone who gives money to help another person; usually someone who supports an artist or writer

retrospective exhibition focused on an artist's past work; looking back or directed in the past

terra-cotta hard, reddish-brown earthenware used for pottery or sculpture

Resources

List of famous works

Richmond Barthe (1901–1989)
Blackberry Woman, 1932
African Dancer, 1933

Aaron Douglas (1899–1979)
Aspects of Negro Life murals, 1934
Build Thee More Stately Mansions, 1944

Palmer Hayden (1890–1973)
The Schooners, c. 1926
The Subway, c. 1930
The Janitor Who Paints a Picture, 1939
The John Henry Series, 1944–1947

Malvin Gray Johnson (1896–1934)
Negro Masks, 1932
Self-Portrait, 1934
Roll Jordan, Roll, c. 1930

Sargent Claude Johnson (1896–1934)
Sammy, 1927
Elizabeth Gee, 1927
Mother and Child, 1932–1933

William H. Johnson (1901–1970)
Going to Church, 1940–1944
Self-Portrait, 1929
Jacobia Hotel, 1930
Jim, 1930

Lois Mailou Jones (1905–1998)
Jennie, 1943
Negro Cabin, Sedalia, North Carolina, 1930
The Ascent of Ethiopia, 1932
Les Fetiches, 1938

Archibald J. Motley Jr. (1891–1981)
Blues, 1929
The Jockey Club, 1929
Saturday Night Street Scene, 1936

Augusta Savage (1892–1962)
Gamin, 1930
La Citadelle—Freedom, 1930
Lift Every Voice and Sing, 1939

James Van Der Zee (1886–1983)
Victory Parade of 369 Regiment, 1919
Dancer, Harlem, 1925
Portrait Of Couple With Raccoon Coats and Stylish Car, 1932

Hale Aspacio Woodruff (1900–1980
The Banjo Player, 1927
Paris Landscape, 1927
Chartres, 1928
Amistad Mutiny Murals, 1938–1939
The Art of the Negro, 1951

Where to see Harlem Renaissance art

Art Institute of Chicago
www.artic.edu/aic
111 S. Michigan Ave.
Chicago, IL 60603
(312) 443-3600

San Francisco Museum of Modern Art
www.sfmoma.org
151 Third St.
San Francisco, CA 94103
(415) 357-4154

Whitney Museum of American Art
www.whitney.org
945 Madison Ave.
New York City, NY 10021
(212) 570-3676

Further Reading

General art books

Beckett, Wendy. *The Story of Painting.* New York: Dorling Kindersley Publishing, 2000.

Barber, Nicola, and Mary Moore. *The World of Art.* New York: Silver Burdett Press, 1998.

Brommer, Gerald F. *Discovering Art History.* Worcester, MA: Davis Publications, Inc., 1997.

Brommer, Gerald F. and Nancy Kline. *Exploring Painting.* Worcester, MA: Davis Publications, Inc., 1995.

Cumming, Robert. *Annotated Guides: Art.* New York: Dorling Kindersley Publishing, 1995.

Greenaway, Shirley. *Art: An A–Z Guide.* Danbury, CT: Franklin Watts, 2000.

Grovignon, Brigette. *The Beginner's Guide to Art.* New York: Harry N. Abrams, Inc., 1998.

Grolier Editorial Staff. *Looking at Art.* Danbury, CT: Grolier Educational Books, Inc., 1996.

Hollingsworth, Patricia. *Smart Art: Learning to Classify and Critique Art.* Tucson, AZ: Zephyr Press, 1998.

Books about the Harlem Renaissance

Beckman, Wendy Hart. *Artists and Writers of the Harlem Renaissance.* Berkeley Heights, NJ: Enslow Publishers, Incorporated, 2002.

Braithewaite-Willis, Deborah. *Vanderzee: Photographer 1886–1983.* New York: Harry N. Abrams, Inc., 1998.

Campbell, Mary S., et. al. *Harlem Renaissance: The Art of Black America.* New York: Harry N. Abrams, Inc., 1994.

Chambers, Veronica. *The Harlem Renaissance.* Broomall, PA: Chelsea House Publishers, 1997.

Hardy, P. Steven and Sheila Jackson Hardy. *Extraordinary People of the Harlem Renaissance.* Danbury, CT: Children's Press, 2000.

Kallen, Stuart A. *The Harlem Renaissance.* Edina, MN: ABDO Publishing Company, 2001.

Hill, Christine M. *Langston Hughes: Poet of the Harlem Renaissance.* Berkeley Heights, NJ: Enslow Publishers, Incorporated, 1997.

Kirschke, Amy H. Aaron Douglas: *Art, Race, and the Harlem Renaissance.* Jackson, MS: University Press of Mississippi, 1995.

Powell, Richard and David A. Bailey. *Rhapsodies in Black: Art of the Harlem Renaissance.* Berkeley, CA: University of California Press, 1997.

Raatma, Lucia. *The Harlem Renaissance.* Chanhassen, MN: The Child's World, Incorporated, 2002.

Slovey, Christine. *Harlem Renaissance.* Farmington Hills, MI: Gale Group, 2000.

Index

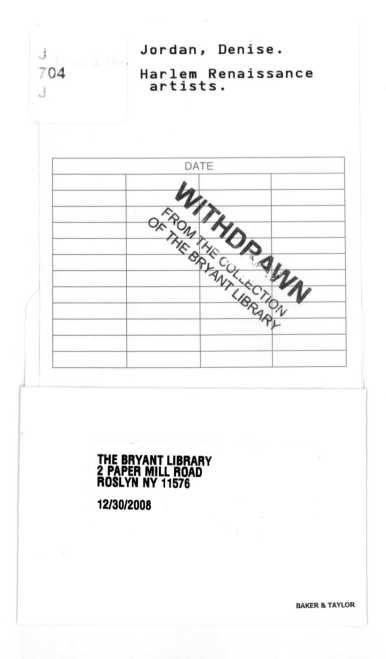